Pre-cut strips & squares make it easy!

Best of Fons&Porter
Quilting Quickly

LEISURE ARTS
the art of everyday living
www.leisurearts.com

FROM MARIANNE & LIZ

We're thrilled to bring you this collection of quilts made from pre-cuts! The projects we've included are all made from strips and squares. They're easy to complete and won't take much time, either. Enjoy the beautiful photography as you browse through the pages to find the quilt that's just right for you. Whether you prefer traditional or contemporary fabrics, you'll find plenty to love. There's also a classroom section that will guide you via step-by-step photography through some basic quilting techniques. We think you'll have fun stitching these beautiful quilts to use in your home or to give as gifts to family and friends.

HAPPY QUILTING,

Marianne + Liz

FONS & PORTER STAFF
Editors-in-Chief Marianne Fons and Liz Porter

Editor Jean Nolte
Managing Editor Debra Finan
Associate Editor Diane Tomlinson
Technical Writer Kristine Peterson

Art Director Kelsey Wolfswinkel

Interactive Editor Morgan Abel
Sewing Specialists Cindy Hathaway, Colleen Tauke
Contributing Photographers Dean Tanner, Kathryn Gamble
Contributing Photo Assistants Mary Mouw

Publisher Kristi Loeffelholz
Advertising Manager Cristy Adamski
Retail Manager Sharon Hart
Web Site Manager Phillip Zacharias
Fons & Porter Staff Shelle Goodwin, Sheyenne Manning, Anne Welker, Karla Wesselmann, Tony Jacobson

New Track Media LLC
President and CEO Stephen J. Kent
Chief Financial Officer Mark F. Arnett
President, Book Publishing W. Budge Wallis
Vice President/Group Publisher Tina Battock
Vice President, Circulation Nicole McGuire
Vice President, Production Barbara Schmitz
Production Manager Dominic M. Taormina
IT Manager Denise Donnarumma
Renewal and Billing Manager Nekeya Dancy
Online Subscriptions Manager Jodi Lee

Our Mission Statement
Our goal is for you to enjoy making quilts as much as we do.

LEISURE ARTS STAFF
Vice President of Editorial Susan White Sullivan
Creative Art Director Katherine Laughlin
Publications Director Leah Lampirez
Special Projects Director Susan Frantz Wiles
Prepress Technician Stephanie Johnson

President and Chief Executive Officer Rick Barton
Senior Vice President of Operations Jim Dittrich
Vice President of Finance Fred F. Pruss
Vice President of Sales-Retail Books Martha Adams
Vice President of Mass Market Bob Bewighouse
Vice President of Technology and Planning Laticia Mull Dittrich
Controller Tiffany P. Childers
Information Technology Director Brian Roden
Director of E-Commerce Mark Hawkins
Manager of E-Commerce Robert Young
Retail Customer Service Manager Stan Raynor

Library of Congress Control Number: 2013957631
ISBN-13/EAN: 978-1-4647-1488-7
UPC: 0-28906-06270-0

PROJECTS

LEARN

8

4

40

INTERMEDIATE

Size: 82½" × 96"
Blocks: 30 (13½") Dresden Plate blocks
Quilt by Jenny Doan of Missouri Star Quilt Co.

DRESDEN BOTANICA

Designer Jenny Doan says, "I love the Dresden and never thought I would own one. Then I found out how easy they are. You just sew straight across the top of the wedge and it makes its own point!"

Quilting Quickly

CUTTING

Measurements include ¼" seam allowances. Border strips are exact length needed. You may want to cut them longer to allow for piecing variations. Wedge and Circle patterns are on page 7. Make template for Inner Circle from heat resistant material (Templar™ or cardboard).

From 5½" × 22" rectangles, cut:
- 600 (5½") Wedges (*Wedge Cutting Diagrams*).

From cream solid, cut:
- 10 (14"-wide) strips. From strips, cut 30 (14") background squares.

NOTE: If cream solid fabric is not 42" wide, cut 15 (14"-wide) strips. From strips, cut 30 (14") background squares.

From tan print, cut:
- 30 Circles.

From purple print, cut:
- 4 (8"-wide) **lengthwise** strips. From strips, cut 2 (8" × 83") top and bottom borders and 2 (8" × 81½") side borders.

From dark purple print, cut:
- 10 (2½"-wide) strips for binding.

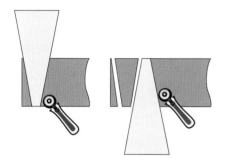

Wedge Cutting Diagrams

Sew Smart

Templates are exact size to use with pre-cuts for less waste.

DRESDEN PLATE BLOCK ASSEMBLY

1. Fold 1 Wedge in half lengthwise, right sides facing. Stitch as shown in *Stitching Diagrams*.

2. Trim corner. Open seam and turn point right side out. Press, centering seam as shown in *Wedge Diagram*. Make 600 wedges.

3. Join 20 wedges to make a Dresden Plate as shown in *Dresden Plate Assembly Diagram* on page 6.

4. Lightly press 1 cream background square in quarters to mark placement lines. Using creases as a guide, center Dresden Plate on square; pin in place (*Block Assembly Diagram* on page 6).

5. Make a gathering stitch around 1 Circle about ⅛" inside edge. Place Inner Circle template on wrong side of circle. Pull thread to gather. Press Circle; remove template.

6. Center prepared Circle on Dresden Plate; pin in place.

7. Appliqué Plate and Circle to background square to complete 1 Dresden Plate block (*Block Diagram* on page 6). Make 30 blocks.

Materials

NOTE: Fabrics in the quilt shown are from the Arabella Rose collection by Marianne Elizabeth for RJR Fabrics.

- 55 (5½" × 22") strips assorted prints in green, purple, rust, tan, and brown
- 4 yards cream solid for block background (6 yards if fabric is less than 42" wide)
- ¾ yard tan print for Circles
- Template material
- MSQC Layer Cake/Charm Pack Dresden Plate Template (optional)
- 2½ yards purple print for border
- ¾ yard dark purple print for binding
- 7½ yards backing fabric
- Queen-size quilt batting

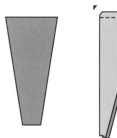

Stitching Diagrams

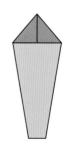

Wedge Diagram

Dresden Plate Assembly Diagram

QUILT ASSEMBLY

1. Lay out blocks as shown in *Quilt Top Assembly Diagram*. Join blocks into rows; join rows to complete quilt center.

2. Add purple print top and bottom side borders to quilt center. Add purple print top and bottom borders to quilt.

FINISHING

1. Divide backing into 3 (2½-yard) lengths. Join panels lengthwise. Seams will run horizontally.

2. Layer backing, batting, and quilt top; baste. Quilt as desired.

3. Join 2½"-wide dark purple print strips into 1 continuous piece for straight-grain French-fold binding. Add binding to quilt. ✦

Sew Smart

When joining wedges, layer 2 wedges, right sides facing. Stitch from top of wedge to bottom.

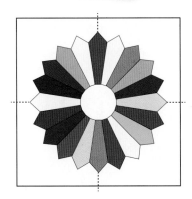

Block Assembly Diagram

Block Diagram

Quilt Top Assembly Diagram

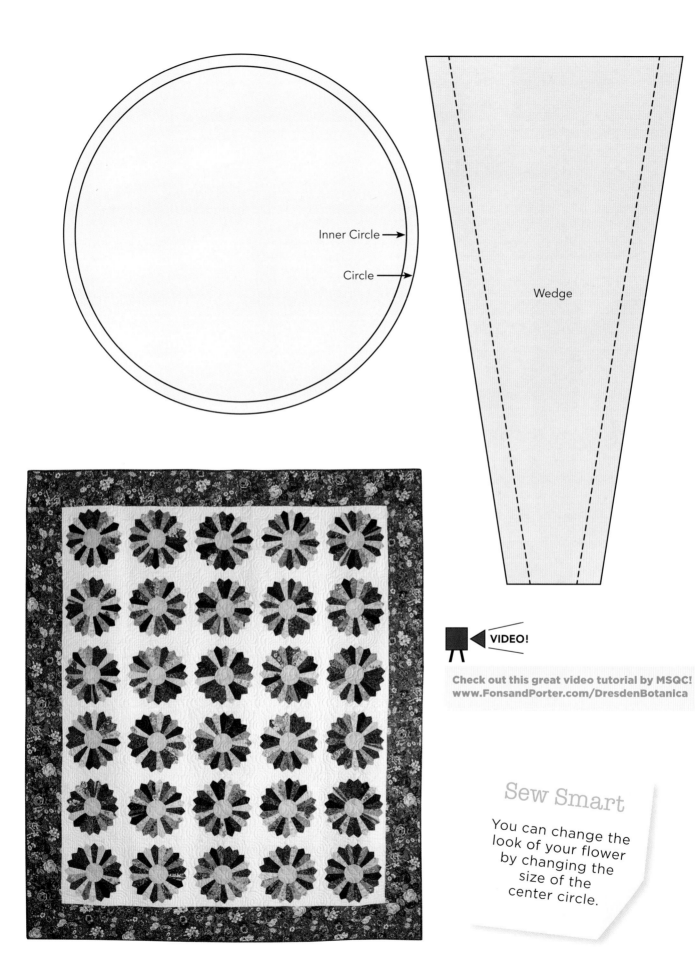

Inner Circle →

Circle →

Wedge

VIDEO!

Check out this great video tutorial by MSQC!
www.FonsandPorter.com/DresdenBotanica

Sew Smart

You can change the look of your flower by changing the size of the center circle.

Size: 81" × 89"
Blocks: 72 (8") Jelly Basket blocks
Quilt by Natalie Earnheart of Missouri Star Quilt Co.

Jelly Basket

Strips and squares combine to make an easy block. Weave the blocks together by placing every other one on its side, and your jelly basket appears.

CUTTING

Measurements include ¼" seam allowances. Border strips are exact length needed; you may want to make them longer to allow for piecing variations.

From assorted print squares, cut:
- 72 (5" × 10") A rectangles (*Cutting Diagram*).

From gray solid, cut:
- 27 (2½"-wide) strips. Piece 9 strips to make 2 (2½" × 77") side inner borders and 2 (2½" × 72½") top and bottom inner borders. From remaining strips, cut 72 (2½" × 10") B rectangles.

From blue solid, cut:
- 28 (2½"-wide) strips. From 18 strips, cut 72 (2½" × 10") B rectangles. Remaining strips are for binding.

From gray print, cut:
- 9 (3½"-wide) strips. Piece strips to make 2 (3½" × 84") side outer borders and 2 (3½" × 81½") top and bottom outer borders.

From yellow print, cut:
- 9 (2"-wide) strips. Piece strips to make 2 (2" × 81") side middle borders and 2 (2" × 75½") top and bottom middle borders.

Materials

NOTE: Fabrics in the quilt shown are from the Bella collection by Windham.

36 (10") assorted print squares

2 yards gray solid for blocks and inner border

1 yard gray print for outer border

⅝ yard yellow print for middle border

2⅛ yards blue solid for blocks and binding

7½ yards backing fabric

Full-size quilt batting

5"

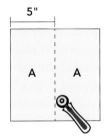

Cutting Diagram

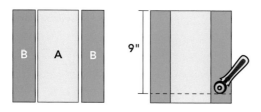

Block Assembly Diagrams

Block Diagram

JELLY BASKET BLOCK ASSEMBLY

1. Lay out 1 print A rectangle and 2 matching B rectangles as shown in *Block Assembly Diagrams*. Join rectangles to make 1 block.

2. Trim block to 9" square as shown to complete 1 Jelly Basket block (*Block Diagram*). Make 72 Jelly Basket blocks.

QUILT ASSEMBLY

1. Lay out Jelly Basket blocks as shown in *Quilt Top Assembly Diagram*. Join into rows; join rows to complete quilt center.

2. Add gray side inner borders to quilt center. Add gray top and bottom inner borders to quilt.

3. Repeat for yellow print middle borders and gray print outer borders.

FINISHING

1. Divide backing into 3 (2½-yard) lengths. Cut 1 piece in half lengthwise to make 2 narrow panels. Join 1 wider panel to each side of narrow panel. Seams will run horizontally. Remaining narrow panel is extra and can be used to make a hanging sleeve.

2. Layer backing, batting, and quilt top; baste. Quilt as desired.

3. Join 2½"-wide blue strips into 1 continuous piece for straight-grain French-fold binding. Add binding to quilt. ✛

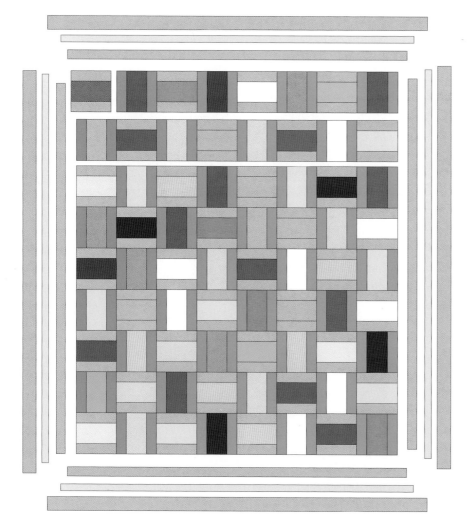

Quilt Top Assembly Diagram

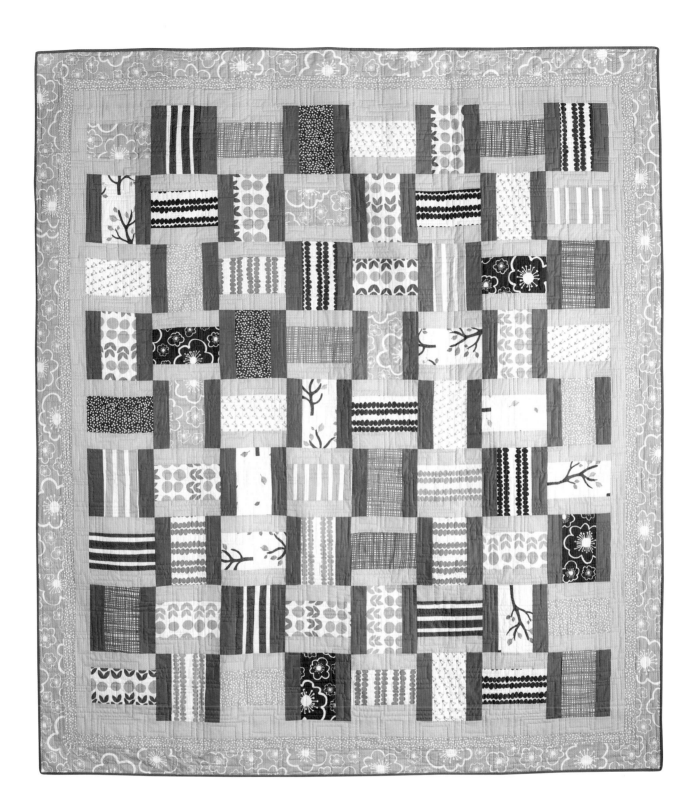

 VIDEO! Check out this great video tutorial by MSQC!
www.FonsandPorter.com/JellyBasket

Size: 58½" × 71"
Blocks: 48" (5¼") blocks
*QUILT BY Jenny Doan of
Missouri Star Quilt Co.*

Playful Pinwheels

Quick and easy to make, these pinwheels will brighten any youngster's room.
Try our super-duper technique for making triangle-squares!

CUTTING

Measurements include ¼" seam allowances. Border strips are exact length
needed. You may want to make them longer to allow for piecing variations.

From white solid, cut:

- 6 (5"-wide) strips. From strips, cut 48 (5") A squares.
- 21 (2½"-wide) strips. From 8 strips, cut 48 (2½" × 5¾") vertical sashing
  rectangles. Piece remaining strips to make 2 (2½" × 56½") side inner
  borders, 2 (2½" × 48") top and bottom inner borders, and 7 (2½" × 44")
  horizontal sashing rectangles.

From multicolor print, cut:

- 7 (6"-wide) strips. Piece strips to make 2 (6" × 60½") side outer borders and
  2 (6" × 59") top and bottom outer borders.

From multicolor stripe, cut:

- 8 (2½"-wide) strips for binding.

MATERIALS

NOTE: Fabrics in the quilt
shown are from the Hello Sunshine
collection by Lori Whitlock for Riley
Blake Designs.

48 (5") assorted print squares

2½ yards white solid

1½ yards multicolor print
for border

¾ yard multicolor stripe for binding

4 yards backing fabric

Twin-size quilt batting

BLOCK ASSEMBLY

1. Place 1 white A square atop 1 print 5" square, right sides facing, as shown in
   Triangle-Square Diagrams. Stitch around perimeter of square, ¼" from edge.
   Cut stitched square in half diagonally in both directions. Press open to reveal
   4 matching Triangle-Squares.

2. Lay out Triangle-Squares as shown in *Block Assembly Diagram.* Join into rows;
   join rows to complete 1 block (*Block Diagram*).

3. Repeat steps #1–#2 to make 48 blocks.

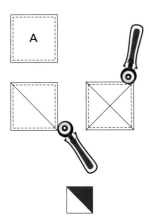

Triangle-Square Diagrams

Block Assembly Diagram

Block Diagram

Quilt Top Assembly Diagram

QUILT ASSEMBLY

1. Lay out blocks and sashing rectangles as shown in *Quilt Top Assembly Diagram*. Join into rows; join rows to complete quilt center.

2. Add white side inner borders to quilt center. Add white top and bottom inner borders to quilt.

3. Repeat for multicolor print outer borders.

FINISHING

1. Divide backing into 2 (2-yard) lengths. Join panels lengthwise. Seam will run horizontally.

2. Layer backing, batting, and quilt top; baste. Quilt as desired.

3. Join 2½"-wide stripe strips into 1 continuous piece for straight-grain French-fold binding. Add binding to quilt. ✛

 VIDEO! Check out this great video tutorial by MSQC!
www.FonsandPorter.com/PlayPin

Size: 86" × 98½"
Blocks: 42 (12½") blocks
*Quilt by Jenny Doan of
Missouri Star Quilt Co.*

BY THE SEA

Try this quick and easy way to make four triangle-squares in one fell swoop. Produce a whole wave of them and your quilt will be almost done.

CUTTING

Measurements include ¼" seam allowances. Border strips are exact length needed; you may want to make them longer to allow for piecing variations.

From blue print #1, cut:
- 9 (6"-wide) strips. Piece strips to make 2 (6" × 88") side borders and 2 (6" × 86½") top and bottom borders.

From blue print #2, cut:
- 10 (2½"-wide) strips for binding.

BLOCK ASSEMBLY

1. Place 1 white square atop 1 blue print square, right sides facing, as shown in *Triangle-Square Diagrams*. Stitch around perimeter of square, ¼" from edge. Cut stitched square in half diagonally in both directions. Press open to reveal 4 Triangle-Squares. Repeat to make 168 Triangle-Squares.

2. Lay out 4 Triangle-Squares with matching-value blues as shown in *Block Assembly Diagram*; join to complete 1 block (Block Diagram). Make 42 blocks.

Materials

NOTE: Fabrics in the quilt shown are from the Seascape collection by Moda.

42 (10") assorted blue print squares

42 (10") white squares

1⅝ yards blue print #1 for border

⅞ yard blue print #2 for binding

7⅞ yards backing fabric

Queen-size quilt batting

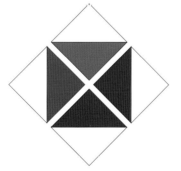

Triangle-Square Diagrams

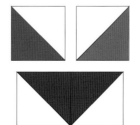

Block Assembly Diagram

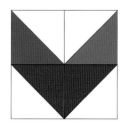

Block Diagram

QUILT ASSEMBLY

1. Lay out blocks as shown in Quilt Top Assembly Diagram. Join into rows; join rows to complete quilt center.

2. Add blue print #1 side borders to quilt center. Add blue print #1 top and bottom borders to quilt.

FINISHING

1. Divide backing into 3 (2⅝-yard) lengths. Join panels lengthwise. Seams will run horizontally.

2. Layer backing, batting, and quilt top; baste. Quilt as desired.

3. Join 2½"-wide blue print #2 strips into 1 continuous piece for straight-grain French-fold binding. Add binding to quilt.

Quilt Top Assembly Diagram

 VIDEO! Check out this great video tutorial by MSQC!
www.FonsandPorter.com/ByTheSea

Size: 38" × 42½"
Blocks: 42 (5") Squares
Quilt by Jenny Doan of
Missouri Star Quilt Co.

Small Charm Quilt

When time is short you can start and finish this darling little quilt in one day.

CUTTING

Measurements include ¼" seam allowances. Border strips are exact length needed; you may want to make them longer to allow for piecing variations.

From cream print, cut:
- 9 (2½"-wide) strips. From 4 strips, cut 2 (2½" × 32") side inner borders and 2 (2½" × 31½") top and bottom inner borders. Remaining strips are for binding.

From brown print, cut:
- 4 (4"-wide) strips. From strips, cut 2 (4" × 36") side outer borders and 2 (4" × 38½") top and bottom outer borders.

QUILT ASSEMBLY

1. Lay out 42 assorted print squares as shown in *Quilt Top Assembly Diagram* on page 22. Join into rows; join rows to complete quilt center.

2. Add cream print side inner borders to quilt center. Add cream print top and bottom inner borders to quilt.

3. Repeat for brown print outer borders.

FINISHING

1. Divide backing into 2 (1¼-yard) lengths. Cut 1 piece in half lengthwise to make 2 narrow panels. Join 1 narrow panel to wider panel. Remaining panel is extra and can be used to make a hanging sleeve.

2. Layer backing, batting, and quilt top; baste. Quilt as desired.

3. Join 2½"-wide cream print strips into 1 continuous piece for straight-grain French-fold binding. Add binding to quilt.

Materials

NOTE: Fabrics in the quilt shown are from the Incense & Peppermints collection by Robin Pandolph for RJR.

42 (5") assorted print squares

¾ yard cream print for inner border and binding

½ yard brown print for outer border

2½ yards backing fabric

Crib-size quilt batting

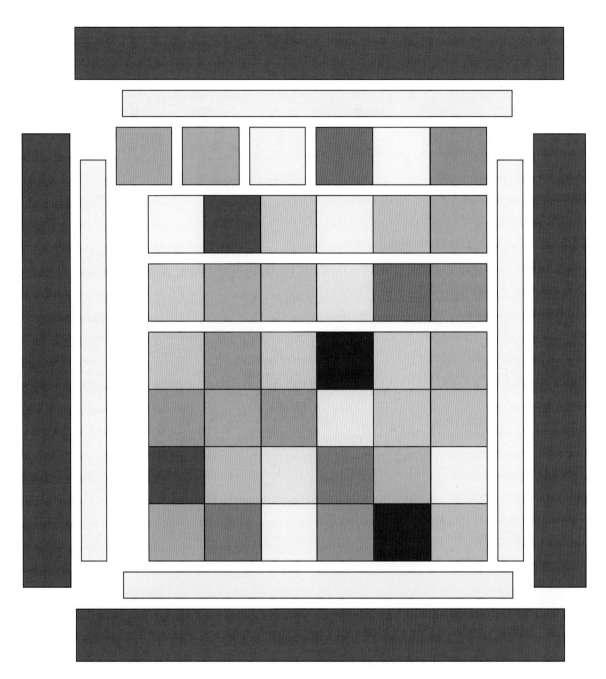

Quilt Top Assembly Diagram

Sew Smart

Never wash pre-cuts before sewing, especially 2½" strips!

 VIDEO! **Check out this great video tutorial by MSQC!**
www.FonsandPorter.com/SmallCharmQuilt

Size: 22"-diameter
Quilt by Jenny Doan of Missouri Star Quilt Co.

HARD CANDY

Incredibly adorable and quick to make, these clever Dresden Plate table toppers are great for dressing up garden furniture or an informal table setting.

CUTTING

Measurements include ¼" seam allowances. Wedge and Circle patterns are on pages 26 and 27. Make template for Inner Circle from heat resistant material (Templar™ or cardboard).

From chevron print, cut:
- 10 (10") Wedges.

From white solid, cut:
- 10 (10") Wedges.

From coordinating fabric, cut:
- 80" of 2½"-wide bias strips for binding.
- 1 Circle.

Materials

NOTE: Fabrics in the quilt shown are Chevron prints by Riley Blake Designs. Materials listed are for one table topper.

⅜ yard chevron print

⅜ yard white solid

½ yard coordinating solid fabric for center and binding

¾ yard backing fabric

26" square quilt batting

MSQC Layer Cake Dresden Plate Template or template material

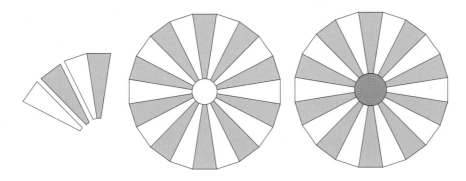

Table Topper Assembly Diagrams

TABLE TOPPER ASSEMBLY

1. Join Wedges as shown in *Table Topper Assembly Diagrams* on page 24. When joining wedges, layer 2 wedges, right sides facing. Stitch from wide end of wedge to narrow end.

2. Make a gathering stitch around Circle about ¼" inside edge. Place Inner Circle template on wrong side of circle. Pull thread to gather. Press Circle; remove template.

3. Center prepared Circle on pieced wedges; pin in place.

4. Appliqué Circle to pieced wedges to complete table topper.

FINISHING

1. Layer backing, batting, and quilt top; baste. Quilt as desired.

2. Add bias binding to quilt. ✚

 VIDEO!

Check out this great video tutorial by MSQC!
www.FonsandPorter.com/HardCandy

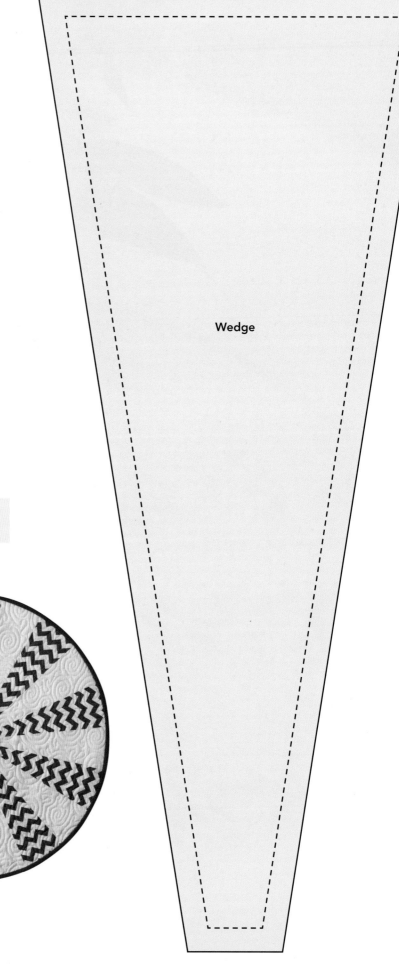

Wedge

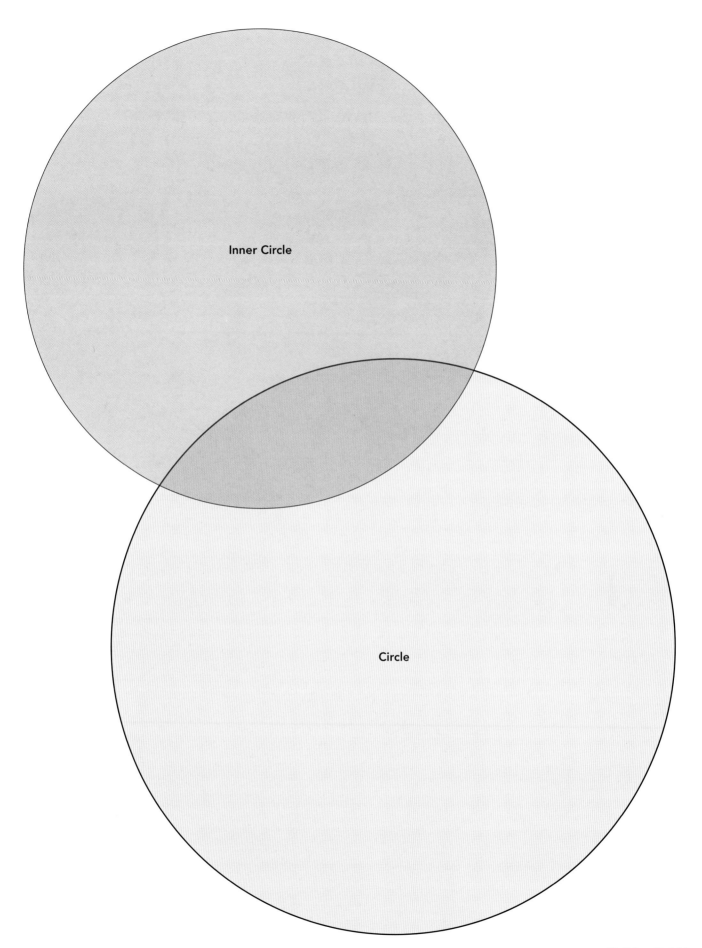

Inner Circle

Circle

Size: 86" × 98"
Blocks: 42 (12") blocks
Quilt by Natalie Earnheart of Missouri Star Quilt Co.

Periwinkle

Inspired by an antique quilt pattern, Natalie used her Wacky Web Triangle Papers to speed up the piecing process in her modern-day version. Watch the Periwinkle video to see what a reversal of white and color spaces does with this pattern!

CUTTING

Measurements include ¼" seam allowances. Border strips are exact length needed. You may want to make them longer to allow for piecing variations. Pattern for Wedge is on page 30.

From each 5" square, cut:
• 1 Wedge.

From white solid, cut:
• 42 (6½"-wide) strips. From strips, cut 336 (6½" × 5") rectangles.

From light blue print, cut:
• 9 (7½"-wide) strips. Piece strips to make 2 (7½" × 84½") side borders and 2 (7½" × 86½") top and bottom borders.

From blue print, cut:
• 10 (2½"-wide) strips for binding.

TRIANGLE UNIT ASSEMBLY

NOTE: If not using Wacky Web Triangle Papers, cut 84 (9½") squares of paper in half diagonally to make 168 paper foundation triangles.

1. Place 1 print Wedge atop 1 paper triangle as shown in *Triangle Unit Diagrams*.

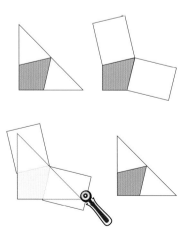

Triangle Unit Diagrams

Materials

NOTE: Fabrics in the quilt shown are from the Honey Honey collection by Kate Spain for Moda Fabrics.

168 (5") assorted blue, orange, pink, and green print squares

8 yards white solid

2¼ yards light blue for border

1 yard blue print for binding

Template material

Wacky Web Triangle Papers (optional)

Glue stick (optional)

8¼ yards backing fabric

Queen-size quilt batting

Sew Smart

Use a dab of glue stick on Triangle Paper to hold fabric Wedge in place.

2. Foundation piece 2 white rectangles to side edges of Wedge shape.

3. Trim pieced triangle even with edges of paper triangle to complete 1 Triangle Unit. Make 168 Triangle Units. Remove papers.

BLOCK ASSEMBLY

1. Lay out 4 Triangle Units as shown in *Block Assembly Diagram*. Join Triangle Units to complete 1 block (*Block Diagram*).

2. Make 42 blocks.

QUILT ASSEMBLY

1. Lay out blocks as shown in *Quilt Top Assembly Diagram*. Join blocks into rows; join rows to complete quilt center.

2. Add light blue print side borders to quilt center. Add light blue print top and bottom borders to quilt.

FINISHING

1. Divide backing into 3 (2¾-yard) lengths. Join panels lengthwise. Seams will run horizontally.

2. Layer backing, batting, and quilt top; baste. Quilt as desired.

3. Join 2½"-wide blue print strips into 1 continuous piece for straight-grain French-fold binding. Add binding to quilt. ✛

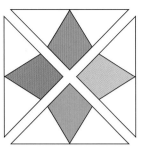

Block Assembly Diagram

Block Diagram

Sew Smart
Remove paper foundation before joining Triangle Units.

Sew Smart
Spray-starch edges of Triangle Units and press before joining.

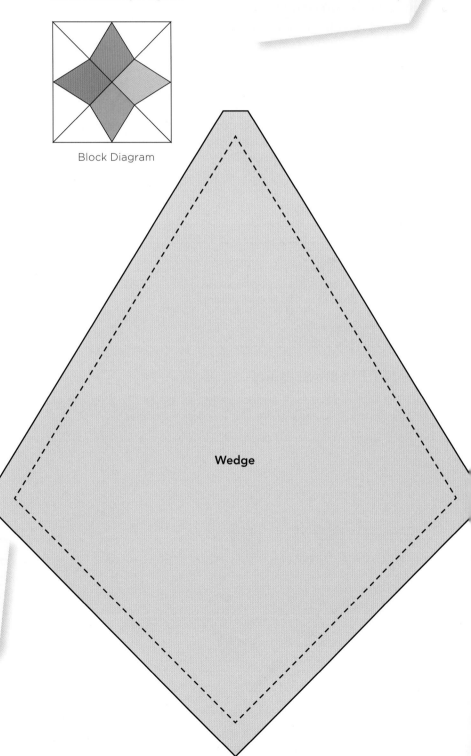

Wedge

Check out this great video tutorial by MSQC!
www.FonsandPorter.com/Periwinkle

Quilt Top Assembly Diagram

INTERMEDIATE

Size: 57" × 73"
Blocks: 18 (8") Sixteen Patch blocks,
17 (8") V blocks
*Quilt by Natalie Earnheart of
Missouri Star Quilt Co.*

Sunny Skies

Learn how to use diagonal seams to get a two-color block—we used blue and white for a sky-like effect. The big colorful patch units shine like a thousand suns.

CUTTING

Measurements include ¼" seam allowances.

From blue print, cut:

- 12 (4½"-wide) strips. From strips, cut 96 (4½") A squares.
- 7 (2½"-wide) strips for binding.

From cream solid, cut:

- 6 (8½"-wide) strips. From strips, cut 48 (8½" × 4½") B rectangles.

From black print, cut:

- 7 (5"-wide) strips. Piece strips to make 2 (5" × 64½") side borders and 2 (5" × 57½") top and bottom borders.

FOUR PATCH UNIT ASSEMBLY

1. Join 2 assorted print strips as shown in *Strip Set Diagrams*.

   Make 12 strip sets.

2. From strip sets, cut 96 (5"-wide) segments.

Materials

NOTE: Fabrics in the quilt shown are from the Chicopee collection by Denyse Schmidt for FreeSpirit Fabrics.

24 (2½" × 44") assorted print strips

2⅛ yards blue print

1½ yards cream solid

1⅛ yards black print for border

3½ yards backing fabric

Twin-size quilt batting

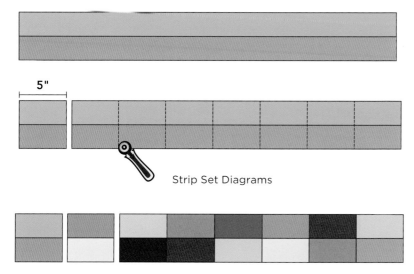

5"

Strip Set Diagrams

Pieced Strip Diagram

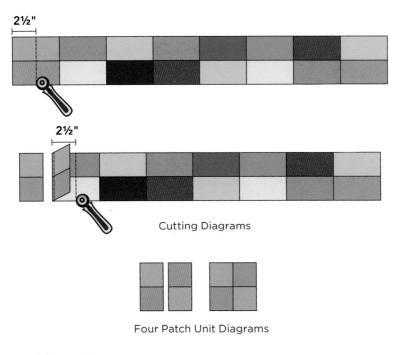

2½"

2½"

Cutting Diagrams

Four Patch Unit Diagrams

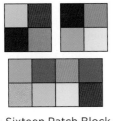

Sixteen Patch Block
Assembly Diagram

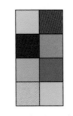

Sixteen Patch
Block Diagram

Eight Patch
Block Diagram

A   B

Make 24

Make 24

Diagonal Seams
Unit Diagrams

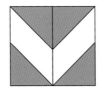

V Block
Assembly Diagram

V Block Diagram

Sew Smart

Mark your diagonal stitching line by pressing square in half diagonally.

3. Join 8 segments to make 1 Pieced Strip (*Pieced Strip Diagram*). Make 12 Pieced Strips.

4. Referring to *Cutting Diagrams*, cut 1 (2½"-wide) segment.

5. Fold remaining half of first segment, right sides facing, over next segment in Pieced Strip. Cut 1 (2½"-wide) section, cutting along previously cut edge of Pieced Strip. Press section open to reveal 1 Four Patch Unit.

6. Continue in this manner, folding Pieced Strip and cutting 2½"-wide sections to make 2 segments and 7 Four Patch Units.

7. Repeat for remaining Pieced Strips.

8. Join 2 segments as shown in *Four Patch Unit Diagrams*. Make 12 Four Patch Units.

9. Lay out 4 Four Patch Units as shown in *Sixteen Patch Block Assembly Diagram*; join to complete 1 Sixteen Patch block (*Sixteen Patch Block Assembly Diagram*). Make 18 Sixteen Patch blocks.

10. Join 2 Four Patch Units to complete 1 Eight Patch block (*Eight Patch Block Diagram*). Make 10 Eight Patch blocks.

V BLOCK ASSEMBLY

1. Press 1 blue print A square in half diagonally, wrong sides facing. Referring to *Diagonal Seams Unit Diagrams*, place pressed square atop 1 cream B rectangle, right sides facing. Stitch diagonally on pressed line, from corner to corner, as shown. Trim ¼" beyond stitching. Press open to reveal triangle. Repeat for opposite end of rectangle to complete 1 Unit. Make 24 Diagonal Seams Units.

2. Repeat to make 24 Diagonal Seams Units with blue print triangles in opposite corners.

3. Lay out 2 Diagonal Seams Units as shown in *V Block Assembly Diagram*. Join to complete 1 V block (*V Block Diagram*). Make 17 V blocks.

QUILT ASSEMBLY

1. Lay out blocks, remaining Four Patch Units, and remaining Diagonal Seams Units as shown in *Quilt Top Assembly Diagram*. Join into rows; join rows to complete quilt center.

2. Add black print side borders to quilt center. Add black print top and bottom borders to quilt.

FINISHING

1. Divide backing into 2 (1¾-yard) lengths. Join panels lengthwise. Seam will run horizontally.

2. Layer backing, batting, and quilt top; baste. Quilt as desired.

3. Join 2½"-wide blue print strips into 1 continuous piece for straight-grain French-fold binding. Add binding to quilt. +

Sew Smart

As often as you can, press seam allowances toward darker fabrics.

Quilt Top Assembly Diagram

 **VIDEO!**

Check out this great video tutorial by MSQC!
www.FonsandPorter.com/SunnySkies

Size: 94" × 121"
Blocks: 12 (25") blocks
Quilt by Jenny Doan and Natalie Earnheart of Missouri Star Quilt Co.

Dashing Stars

Using triangle-squares and snowball corners, you'll piece together this large quilt in no time.

CUTTING

Measurements include ¼" seam allowances. Border strips are exact length needed. You may want to cut them longer to allow for piecing variations.

From each of 12 assorted light or dark print 10" squares, cut:
- 4 (5") A squares.

From brown print, cut:
- 11 (2½"-wide) strips. From 1 strip, cut 6 (2½") C squares. Piece remaining strips to make 2 (2½" × 106½") side inner borders and 2 (2½" × 83½") top and bottom inner borders.

From red print, cut:
- 12 (6"-wide) strips. Piece strips to make 2 (6" × 110½") side outer borders and 2 (6" × 94½") top and bottom outer borders.
- 12 (2½"-wide) strips for binding.

From ecru solid, cut:
- 8 (6¾"-wide) strips. From strips, cut 48 (6¾") B squares.
- 12 (2½"-wide) strips. Piece strips to make 17 (2½" × 25½") D rectangles.

BLOCK ASSEMBLY

1. Place 1 ecru 10" square atop 1 light 10" square, right sides facing, as shown in *Triangle-Square Diagrams*. Stitch around perimeter of square, ¼" from edge. Cut stitched square in half diagonally in both directions. Press open to reveal 4 matching Triangle-Squares.

Materials

NOTE: Fabrics in the quilt shown are from the Orchard House collection by Windham Fabrics.

- 30 (10") assorted light print squares
- 30 (10") assorted dark print squares
- 24 (10") ecru solid squares
- ⅞ yard brown print for inner border
- 3 yards red print for outer border and binding
- 2½ yards ecru solid
- 10⅞ yards backing fabric
- 3½ yards of 120"-wide quilt batting

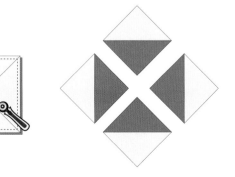

Triangle-Square Diagrams

2. In the same manner, make 4 matching Triangle-Squares using 1 ecru 10" square and 1 dark print 10" square. Make 4 matching Triangle-Squares using 1 light print 10" square and 1 dark print 10" square.

3. Referring to *Corner Unit Diagrams*, press 1 A square in half diagonally, wrong sides facing. Place pressed square atop 1 ecru B square, right sides facing. Stitch diagonally from corner to corner as shown. Trim ¼" beyond stitching. Press open to reveal triangle. Make 4 matching Corner Units.

4. Lay out Triangle-Squares and Corner Units as shown in *Block Assembly Diagram*; join into rows. Join rows to complete 1 block (*Block Diagram*).

5. Repeat steps #1–4 to make 12 blocks.

QUILT ASSEMBLY

1. Lay out blocks, brown print C squares and ecru D rectangles as shown in *Quilt Top Assembly Diagram*. Join into rows; join rows to complete quilt center.

2. Add brown print side inner borders to quilt center. Add brown print top and bottom inner borders to quilt.

3. Repeat for red print outer borders.

FINISHING

1. Divide backing into 3 (3⅝–yard) lengths. Cut 1 piece in half lengthwise to make 2 narrow panels. Join 1 wider panel to each side of narrow panel; press seam allowances toward narrow panel. Remaining panel is extra and can be used to make a hanging sleeve.

2. Layer backing, batting, and quilt top; baste. Quilt as desired.

3. Join 2½"–wide red print strips into 1 continuous piece for straight-grain French-fold binding. Add binding to quilt. ✚

Corner Unit Diagrams

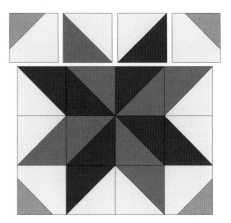

Block Assembly Diagram

Block Diagram

Quilt Top Assembly Diagram

Sew Smart

Sashing with cornerstones works well with any block pattern.

VIDEO!

Check out this great video tutorial by MSQC!
www.FonsandPorter.com/DashingStars

Size: 74" × 83"
Blocks: 42 (9") blocks
Quilt by Jenny Doan of Missouri Star Quilt Co.

X's and O's Quilt

This is an old block pattern made new with pre-cuts! In the old days it was used as a signature block, with the solid in the middle.

CUTTING

From green print, cut:

- 8 (6"-wide) strips. Piece strips to make 2 (6" × 72½") side outer borders and 2 (6" × 74½") top and bottom outer borders.

- 3 (5"-wide) strips. From strips, cut 18 (5") A squares.

- 9 (2½"-wide) strips for binding.

From purple print, cut:
- 9 (5"-wide) strips. From strips, cut 68 (5") A squares.

From each white square, cut:
- 4 (2½") B squares (*Cutting Diagram*).

BLOCK ASSEMBLY

1. Press 1 white B square in half diagonally, wrong sides facing. Place pressed square atop 1 print A square, right sides facing, as shown in *Block Unit Assembly Diagrams*. Stitch diagonally from corner to corner on pressed line as shown. Trim ¼" beyond stitching. Press open to reveal triangle. Repeat for opposite corner of A square to complete 1 Block Unit (*Block Unit Diagram*). Make 138 Block Units.

2. In the same manner, make 12 purple Block Units using 2 white B squares and 1 purple print A square in each, and 18 green Block Units using 2 white B squares and 1 green print square in each.

Materials

NOTE: Fabrics in the quilt shown are from the Garden Medley collection by Benartex.

138 (5") assorted print squares (A)

97 (5") white solid squares

1⅜ yards purple print for blocks, and inner border

2½ yards green print for blocks, outer border, and binding

5 yards backing fabric

Full-size quilt batting

Cutting Diagram

Block Unit Assembly Diagrams

Block Unit Diagram

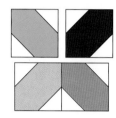

Border Unit Diagram

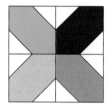

Block Assembly Diagram   Block Diagram

Quilt Top Assembly Diagram

3. In a similar manner, make 52 Border Units, using 1 white B square and 1 purple print A square in each (*Border Unit Diagram*).

4. Lay out 4 Block Units, matching solid to solid and print to print, as shown in *Block Assembly Diagram*; join Units into rows, join rows to complete 1 block (*Block Diagram*). Make 42 blocks.

QUILT ASSEMBLY

1. Lay out blocks as shown in *Quilt Top Assembly Diagram*. Join into rows; join rows to complete quilt center.

2. Join 14 Border Units to complete 1 pieced side inner border as shown in *Quilt Top Assembly Diagram*. Make 2 pieced side inner borders.

3. In the same manner, join 12 Border Units and 2 purple print A squares to complete 1 pieced top inner border. Repeat for pieced bottom inner border.

4. Add pieced side inner borders to quilt center. Add pieced top and bottom inner borders to quilt.

5. Repeat for green print outer borders.

FINISHING

1. Divide backing into 2 (2½-yard) lengths. Cut 1 piece in half lengthwise to make 2 narrow panels. Join 1 narrow panel to each side of wider panel. Press seam allowances toward narrow panels.

2. Layer backing, batting, and quilt top; baste. Quilt as desired.

3. Join 2½"-wide green print strips into 1 continuous piece for straight-grain French-fold binding. Add binding to quilt. ✚

 VIDEO! **Check out this great video tutorial by MSQC!**
www.FonsandPorter.com/XsandOs

Sew Smart

This border technique is an easy way to jazz up any quilt.

Size: 22" × 31"
Blocks: 6 (9") blocks
Quilt by Jenny Doan of Missouri Star Quilt Co.

X's and O's Pillow Sham

This is one of my favorite quilt blocks as it makes an X and O which is like a secret message of hugs and kisses to whomever gets the pillow sham!

CUTTING

From green print, cut:

- 3 (2½"-wide) strips. From strips, cut 2 (2½" × 31½") top and bottom borders and 2 (2½" × 18½") side borders.

From white solid, cut:

- 2 (22½"-wide) strips for pillow back.

- 2 (5"-wide) strips. From strips, cut 12 (5") squares. From each square, cut 4 (2½") B squares (*Cutting Diagram*).

BLOCK ASSEMBLY

1. Press 1 white B square in half diagonally, wrong sides facing. Place pressed square atop 1 print A square, right sides facing, as shown in *Block Unit Assembly Diagrams*. Stitch diagonally from corner to corner on pressed line as shown. Trim ¼" beyond stitching. Press open to reveal triangle. Repeat for opposite corner of A square to complete 1 Block Unit (*Block Unit Diagram*). Make 24 Block Units.

2. Lay out 4 Block Units, matching solid to solid and print to print, as shown in *Block Assembly Diagram*; join to complete 1 block (*Block Diagram*). Make 6 blocks.

Materials

NOTE: Fabrics in the pillow sham shown are from the Garden Medley collection by Benartex.

24 (5") assorted print squares (A)

⅜ yard green print for border

1⅝ yards white solid for blocks and back

¾ yard lining fabric

26" × 35" rectangle quilt batting

Cutting Diagram

Block Unit Assembly Diagrams

Block Unit Diagram

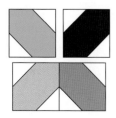

Block Assembly Diagram

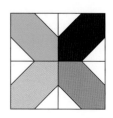

Block Diagram

PILLOW TOP ASSEMBLY

1. Lay out blocks as shown in *Pillow Top Assembly Diagram*. Join into rows; join rows to complete pillow top center.

2. Add green print side borders to pillow top center. Add green print top and bottom borders to pillow top.

FINISHING

1. Layer lining fabric, batting, and pillow top; baste. Quilt as desired.

2. Trim lining and batting even with pillow top. Stay-stitch around perimeter of pillow top, a scant ¼" from edges. Carefully trim away batting from seam allowance.

3. Fold backing rectangles in half crosswise, wrong side facing; press.

4. Overlap pressed edges of pillow back rectangles, making a rectangle same size as pillow top. Baste overlapped edges together (*Pillow Back Diagram*).

5. Place pillow top atop pillow back, right sides facing. Stitch around outer edges. Turn right side out. Insert pillow. ✚

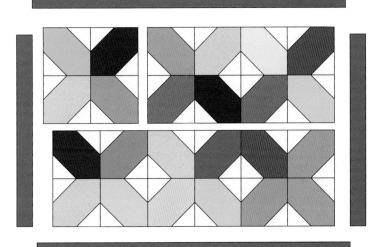

Pillow Top Assembly Diagram

Pillow Back Diagram

Sew Smart

2:1 For any size quilt:
2 charm print squares
for every
1 solid square

Size: 76" × 83¾"
Blocks: 72 (7¾") blocks
*Quilt by Natalie Earnheart of
Missouri Star Quilt Co.*

Summer in the Park

Strip sets and a wicked smart cutting technique make for quick striped blocks. Set the blocks color to color and you'll have a quilt in time for your picnic…in the park.

CUTTING

Measurements include ¼" seam allowances. Border strips are exact length needed. You may want to make them longer to allow for piecing variations. To make template for triangle, cut 8⅜" square of template plastic in half diagonally.

From pink print, cut:
- 8 (5½"-wide) strips. Piece strips to make 2 (5½" × 74½") side outer borders and 2 (5½" × 76½") top and bottom outer borders.
- 9 (2½"-wide) strips for binding.

From cream solid, cut:
- 8 (2½"-wide) strips. Piece strips to make 2 (2½" × 62½") side inner borders and 2 (2½" × 66½") top and bottom inner borders.

BLOCK ASSEMBLY

1. Join 2 assorted print strips and 1 cream strip as shown in *Strip Set #1 Diagram.* Make 13 Strip Set #1.

2. Join 2 cream strips and 1 assorted print strip as shown in *Strip Set #2 Diagram.* Make 13 Strip Set #2.

Materials

NOTE: Fabrics in the quilt shown are from the Gypsy Girl collection by Lily Ashbury for Moda Fabrics.

- 39 (2½" × 44") assorted print strips
- 39 (2½" × 44") cream solid strips
- 2 yards pink print for border and binding
- ⅝ yard cream solid for inner border
- 5¼ yards backing fabric
- 12½" square ruler or template plastic
- Full-size quilt batting

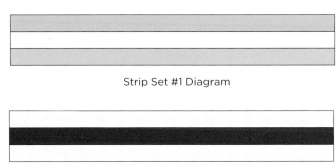

Strip Set #1 Diagram

Strip Set #2 Diagram

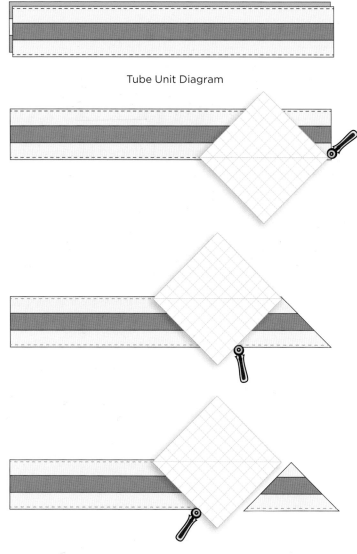

Tube Unit Diagram

Tube Unit Cutting Diagrams

Block Diagram

3. Place 1 Strip Set #2 atop 1 Strip Set #1, right sides facing. Stitch together along long edges to make Tube Unit (*Tube Unit Diagram*). Make 13 Tube Units.

4. Place 12½" square ruler on Tube Unit with diagonal center line on 1 stitched line as shown in *Tube Unit Cutting Diagrams*. Cut away end piece. Move ruler so diagonal center line is on opposite seam line. Cut 1 Pieced Triangle. Continue cutting Tube Units in this manner to make 72 Pieced Triangles.

5. Press open 1 Pieced Triangle to reveal 1 block (*Block Diagram*). Make 72 Blocks.

QUILT ASSEMBLY

1. Lay out blocks as shown in *Quilt Top Assembly Diagram*.

2. Add cream side inner borders to quilt center. Add cream top and bottom inner borders to quilt.

3. Repeat for pink print outer borders.

FINISHING

1. Divide backing into 2 (2⅝-yard) lengths. Cut 1 piece in half lengthwise to make 2 narrow panels. Join 1 narrow panel to each side of wider panel.

2. Layer backing, batting, and quilt top; baste. Quilt as desired.

3. Join 2½"-wide pink print strips into 1 continuous piece for straight-grain French-fold binding. Add binding to quilt. ✚

Sew Smart

Make sure diagonal center line of square ruler is on the seam line, not the edge of the fabric.

Quilt Top Assembly Diagram

 VIDEO!

Check out this great video tutorial by MSQC!
www.FonsandPorter.com/SummerInThePark

Size: 90" × 104"
Quilt by Natalie Earnheart of Missouri Star Quilt Co.

Ingrid's Garden

This is not your grandmother's flower garden! With this easy Half-Hexagon template you get the look without the set-in seams.

CUTTING

Measurements include ¼" seam allowances. Pattern for Half Hexagon is on page 54.

From print squares, cut:
- 156 Half Hexagons as follows: Fold 1 (10") print square in half. Place short edge of Half-Hexagon template along raw edges of fabric (*Cutting Diagrams*). Cut fabric along sides and long edge of template to make 2 Half Hexagons as shown.

From cream solid, cut:
- 11 (10"-wide) strips. Fold strips in half lengthwise. From strips, cut 86 Half Hexagons.
- 9 (2½"-wide) strips. Join strips for inner borders.

NOTE: Inner borders will be cut to correct length after quilt center is assembled.

From pink print, cut:
- 10 (6½"-wide) strips. Join strips for outer borders.

NOTE: Outer borders will be cut to correct length after quilt center is assembled.

From pink stripe, cut:
- 11 (2½"-wide) strips for binding.

Materials

NOTE: Fabrics in the quilt shown are from the Moda Bella Solids line and the Marmalade collection by Bonnie & Camille for Moda Fabrics.

78 (10") assorted print squares

4 yards cream solid

2 yards pink print for border

1 yard pink stripe for binding

8¼ yards backing fabric

MSQC 10" Half-Hexagon Template or template plastic

Queen-size quilt batting

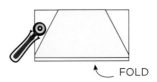

FOLD

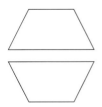

Cutting Diagrams

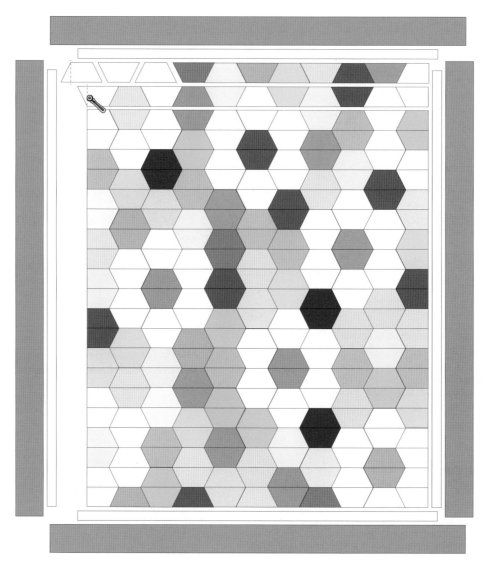

Quilt Top Assembly Diagram

QUILT ASSEMBLY

1. Lay out Half Hexagons as shown in *Quilt Top Assembly Diagram.* Join into rows; join rows to complete quilt center. Trim side edges of quilt center as shown.

2. Measure length of quilt center. Cut 2 cream side inner borders this measurement. Add side inner borders to quilt center.

3. Measure width of quilt center, including side inner borders. Cut 2 cream top and bottom inner borders this measurement. Add top and bottom inner borders to quilt.

4. In the same manner, measure length of quilt, including top and bottom inner borders. Cut 2 pink print side outer borders to this measurement. Add side outer borders to quilt center.

5. Measure width of quilt, including side outer borders. Cut 2 pink top and bottom outer borders this measurement. Add top and bottom outer borders to quilt.

FINISHING

1. Divide backing into 3 (2¾-yard) lengths. Join panels lengthwise. Seams will run horizontally.

2. Layer backing, batting, and quilt top; baste. Quilt as desired.

3. Join 2½"-wide pink stripe strips into 1 continuous piece for straight-grain French-fold binding. Add binding to quilt. ✛

 VIDEO!

Check out this great video tutorial by MSQC!
www.FonsandPorter.com/IngridsGarden

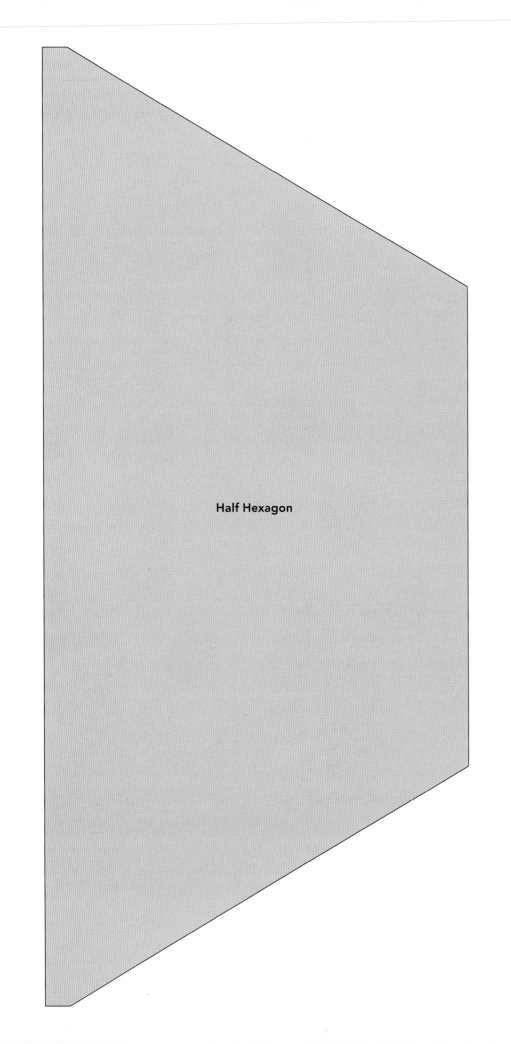

Half Hexagon

pre-cut primer

Pre-cut packaging and naming varies among manufacturers. For example, Moda names their 2½" × 42" strip package a Jelly Roll™ and Riley Blake calls them Rolie Polies.

Each manufacturer decides how many pieces to include in each pack—40 pieces per pack is pretty standard but some companies put in more or less, depending on the number of fabrics a designer has in a collection.

fat quarter bundle

A fat quarter contains the same amount of fabric as a quarter yard. Because it is cut approximately 18" × 22" it is more useful than the standard, narrow 9" × 44" cut. A fat quarter bundle typically has one cut of each fabric in a collection.

Sew Smart

If you are a beginning quilter, using a charm pack is the easiest way to get started. Just sew the squares together, and you'll have a quilt finished in no time!

charm pack™

A charm pack contains 5" charm squares, often containing a small 'taste' of each design in a collection. Usually consisting of about 40 pieces, 1 charm pack will make a baby quilt, 2 charm packs a crib-size quilt, 3 charm packs a lap quilt, and 4–5 charm packs contain enough for a twin-size quilt.

jelly roll™

This package of approximately 40 (2½" × 44") strips can make a lap or small twin-size quilt. Available from a number of manufacturers under a variety of names, the strips are great for making striped triangles or any type of strippy project.

Sew Smart

If pre-cuts are cut with a pinking blade, measure from the outer peak of the pinked edge when cutting or determining seam allowances.

layer cake™

Layer Cakes are collections of 10" × 10" squares of fabric—similar to a charm pack but a larger size. Originally packaged and named by Moda Fabrics, Layer Cakes are available by collection and typically include 42 pieces of fabric, although the number may vary.

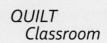
Have you ever wondered what the straight grain is?

Fabric is woven using widthwise threads—from selvedge to selvedge—which we call the weft, and lengthwise threads, which are called the warp. Either direction can refer to the straight of grain. So, threads directly across the fabric or straight down the side of the fabric, are called straight of grain.

Check out this great video tutorial by MSQC!
www.FonsandPorter.com/msqcStraightGrain

Have you ever wondered what a selvedge edge is?

Well, the selvedge edge is the self-finished edge of your fabric. Often the selvedge has valuable information printed on it about the fabric itself, such as the designer, fabric company, pattern identification and, as is the case in the photo, a dot with every color used in that particular fabric. So if your pattern ever mentions the selvedge, now you know!

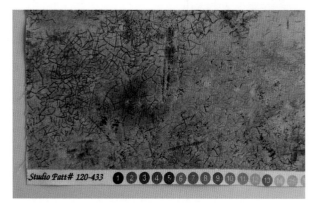

Check out this great video tutorial by MSQC!
www.FonsandPorter.com/msqcSelvedge

Here's the secret of the ironing board so many of you ask about!

1 Gather your supplies:
1. A piece of wood 18″ × 24″ and about ¼″ thick (We used wood floor underlayment.)
2. Bath towel at least twice the size of your piece of wood
3. Fabric to cover the ironing board.

2 Fold the towel in half and stitch up the sides at the width of the board. Put the towel over the board like a pillowcase. No need to buy a new towel—an old towel works just as well!

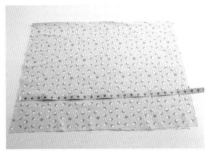

3 Cut a piece of fabric about 40″ × 26″. Make sure it's big enough to cover the towel-wrapped wood piece.

4 Fold the fabric right sides together and sew the side seams with an even little seam—¼″ to ½″ works well. Use a serger to finish the top edge of the cover or, if you prefer, turn a hem.

5 Turn the cover right side out and slide it over the towel-wrapped board.

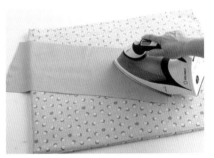

6 In no time you have an ironing board pad just like the one in the video! This works great because you can put it right on your counter. It's the same size as most of the 24″ cutting mats, so you can just take it with you in your bag when you go to class!

 VIDEO! **Check out this great video tutorial by MSQC!**
www.FonsandPorter.com/msqcIroningPad

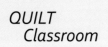
Here's a trick that works well for making triangle-squares, especially if you need lots of them. These are so versatile and so fun!

1 Cut 4 squares, 2 each in contrasting fabrics. Generally, when you make a triangle-square, you draw a pencil line on the back of your square and you sew on either side of that line.

2 Press 2 squares corner to corner, across the block diagonally, creating a guide line so you don't have to spend hours with your ruler and a pencil.

3 Open the pressed squares and lay them on top of the other squares—you can see that the pressed lines are quite visible. Take these to the sewing machine and sew on either side of the pressed lines.

4 Put your presser foot down right on that line and sew along with a 1/4" seam allowance. Either sew the seam on the other side of the line, or just go ahead and place the next pair of squares under the presser foot with the presser foot staying on the line.

5   Using the pressed line as a guide, cut right down the middle with a rotary cutter or scissors—if I had a lot to do I'd use a rotary cutter.

6   With dark sides up, set the seams, then lift the dark side and press out. We've made four triangle-squares in the time it takes to sew two!

7   Now, four triangle-squares can be used for all sorts of things. When you line up your squares with the light towards the middle (A), you make a square we like to call love letters. You can also turn them with the dark to the middle (B), and it gives you a completely different look. Now if you want to make a pinwheel (C), you can do that by placing your darks in a clockwise fashion—pinwheels really are one of America's favorite blocks. If you like, you can keep all your triangle-squares turned the same direction (D). Use triangle-squares to create all kinds of designs.

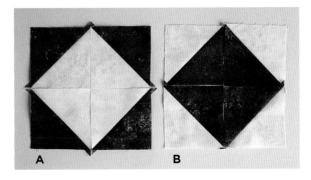

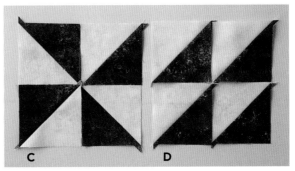

 VIDEO!

Check out this great video tutorial by MSQC!
www.FonsandPorter.com/sqcTriangleSquares

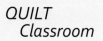

We love tips that make our quilting faster and quicker, and that includes speeding up the actual quilting portion of our quiltmaking.

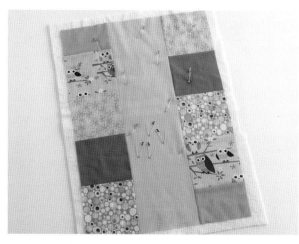

1 Make sure you have the correct supplies. You'll need curved safety pins or temporary basting spray that won't gum up your needle.

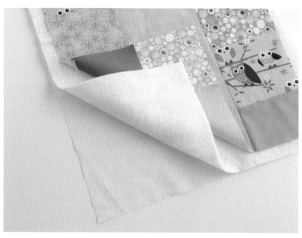

2 Layer your quilt sandwich—make sure your backing and batting are several inches larger than finished top.

3 Spray, or pin-baste, your quilt—spray backing fabric and place batting on top; spray batting and add top, being careful to center on backing and batting. Make sure the layers are all nice and flat.

4 Roll your quilt so it fits in machine throat area. Use an open-toe hopping foot and lower the feed dogs.

◀ VIDEO! **Check out this great video tutorial by MSQC!**
www.FonsandPorter.com/msqcFreeMotion

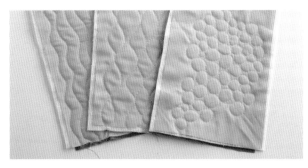

5 Use machine quilting gloves if you want, or just your hands to push the quilt under the needle. Make sure your hands don't move faster than machine is stitching or you will get big stitches. Use the needle down setting if you have one—that will help when you start and stop. Make sample quilt sandwiches to reference.

6 Check your stitching as you go to make sure the tension is set properly and there are no eyelashes or dragon teeth showing on the back.

7 If you used pins for your basting, you need to remove them as you go—do not stitch over them.

8 On small projects, start quilting at one edge. On larger projects, start in the center and do your quilting in quarters.

9 Put binding on a practice sample to make a diaper changing pad.

Here's a quick-and-easy way to sew on a binding using the machine. Just follow the steps here, or watch the video, and learn to finish your quilt.

1 Cut binding strips 2½" wide. Iron the strips in half by folding the edges together with wrong sides facing, and iron the whole length. There are two reasons for this: it makes the binding lie flat and, when joining the strips at a 45-degree angle, it makes it easy to see where the fold lines cross.

2 To join strips, open up the fold, and place one directly across the other so it makes a little cross. It's not necessary to cut off the selvedges because they stick out beyond the edges.

3 Sew from edge to edge, starting and stopping where the two fabrics meet. Join strips with an angled seam so there is less bulk, making the finished binding smoother.

4 To chain piece my binding strips, first sew straight across, then grab the other end of the top strip and position it in front of the needle. Lay the next strip across it, right sides together, and sew across the two; repeat until all strips are joined. Be sure to have enough strips because there's nothing worse than getting to the last side of your quilt and being short on binding!

5 After all the binding strips are chain pieced, cut them apart. Then cut the excess fabric, leaving about ¼" seam allowance. You don't have to cut particularly straight because you sewed straight; when you open your binding, you'll see that it's nice and flat.

6 When attaching your binding by machine, sew it onto the back of the quilt sandwich, bring it around to the front, and put a nice decorative stitch on it. If you do it the opposite way you don't know where that stitch is going to land.

 **VIDEO!** **Check out this great video tutorial by MSQC!**
www.FonsandPorter.com/msqcMachineBinding

7 As you're stitching your binding and get to a corner, stop a little bit more than a ¼" (maybe a ½") from the end.

8 Pull your quilt out of the machine. Fold the binding back, over your thumb, and pull the tail up until the binding meets up with the corner of the quilt.

9 Fold the binding forward so that it lines up with the edge of the quilt, and you're ready to sew down the next side.

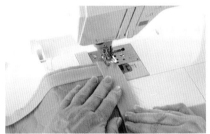

10 Sew to the next corner and repeat the miter process. When you get to the last side, join your binding ends using your favorite method (see our Binding Tool Classroom on page 64!) and finish stitching the binding to the quilt. Trim off excess batting.

11 Now you're ready to stitch the binding to the top. Bring the folded edge of the binding strip to the front and place it along the stitch line; sew with a decorative stitch. Stop every 6" or so to make sure the fold is meeting up with the edge of the stitch line.

12 When you get to the corner, hold down the binding, making sure it's covering the stitch line and goes flat off the edge. Sew to the corner where the stitch lines meet, then with the needle down and presser foot raised, pivot before stitching the next side.

13 Lift up the needle and fold the binding over the stitch line on the next side. Put the needle back down, and you're ready to sew the next side.

14 Be sure to hold the binding edge down at the corner to make sure it makes a nice miter.

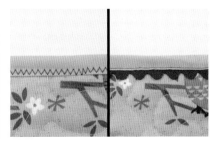

15 Use zigzag or decorative stitches on your binding. This is also a fun place to add trim such as rickrack.

Use this terrific little tool to finish your binding like a pro, without having to fudge and/or fumble your binding ends into submission.

1 Sew binding to quilt, leaving 10" tails, 12" apart. Place flat end of tool at one tail. Mark binding next to "Mark Here" line on tool.

2 Open up the binding and place the line of the binding tool on the mark you just made (where the tool is marked with a B).

3 Trim the binding strip along the angled edge of the binding tool. Trim the little point at the tip which helps you line up the ends when you sew them together.

4 Rotate the tool so the flat edge is on the left; place at second tail. Be sure the printed side of the tool is facing up. Make a mark at the line on this side.

5 This is the place where many people make a mistake. On this side, put the tip (marked A) on the mark you made.

6 Trim the binding strip along the angled edge of the binding tool.

7 Line up the ends of your binding, right sides together.

8 Sew the ends of your binding strips together with a ¼" seam.

9 Fold the joined binding back in half and stitch it to your quilt. It should be a perfect fit!

 VIDEO!

Check out this great video tutorial by MSQC!
www.FonsandPorter.com/msqcBindingTool